sundance
publishing

LITTLE RED
READERS

M000079759

At the Water Hole

PETER SLOAN &
SHERYL SLOAN

A zebra is
at the water hole.

It is drinking.

A giraffe is
at the water hole.

It is drinking.

A lion is
at the water hole.

It is drinking.

A jackal is
at the water hole.

It is drinking.

A leopard is
at the water hole.

It is drinking.

A hyena is
at the water hole.

It is drinking.

A gazelle is
at the water hole.

It is drinking.